CHANGE OF PERCEPTION

Change of Perception

GABRIELE HAUSER

CONTENTS

Contents ~ vii

x ~ *Contents*

Contents ~ xix

Contents ~ xxi

~ 1 ~

On rainy days
l wash my soul
scrub off the stains
left hanging on
and when the sun
comes out again
l hang her neatly
on a line to dry.

~ 2 ~

~ 3 ~

Grace is the wildflower
blooming on the ledge of hope
where thought is rendered speechless
by silent winged forces as of yet
unknown to man.

~ 4 ~

~ 5 ~

I am

my best friend
my worst enemy
my humblest of servant
my worst dictator
my gentle observer
my destructive self
but above it all

l am love.

~ 6 ~

~ 7 ~

Subtle the daytime curtain
draws shut behind the
scurrying steps the setting
sun leaves in her wake
shadows cast their light
into the black tar kettle
of the night, lost souls
and gremlins wake...

...this is their world.

~ 8 ~

~ *9* ~

If you are sanding
down my edges
you will make me
what I don't want to be
and you someone
I can't be with.

~ 10 ~

~ 11 ~

Anger is sadness
turned upside down.

~ 12 ~

~ 13 ~

The thing that hurts
more than losing someone
is being lost to someone.

~ 14 ~

~ 15 ~

Some days are like molasses

dark, golden-brown colored
heavily textured
the flow of melted lava
slowly gliding along the spoon

into the cup.

~ 16 ~

~ 17 ~

The moon lend me his lantern
so I could spread his light
below my footsteps in this dark
and lonely night.

~ 18 ~

~ 19 ~

Time does not exist within her gates
the ruins that I left to memory
the guarded curtain of forgetfulness
wrapped tight around my memories
will free herself of space and time and
render upon me - her tapered sword.

.

~ 20 ~

~ 21 ~

From within
meadow's glisten
roses wilted moments ago
bloom – igniting
in color of light
my world.

~ 22 ~

~ 23 ~

Pain
is easier to endure
looking at it through
the rear-view mirror
then staring it straight
in the face

but only by its stare
are we set free.

~ 24 ~

~ 25 ~

Why would you fear the loss of one love
when the whole world lies at your feet?

~ 26 ~

~ 27 ~

Mornings come
and mornings go
in even cycles
do they flow
between the coming and going
imagination gives
way to yet
unborn creations.

~ 28 ~

~ 29 ~

Change
can bring sorrow

change
can bring pain

change
can render you speechless

change
can make you quiver

and still, change in time

will light your fire.

~ 30 ~

~ 31 ~

To be ignorant to change
might lengthen your trip.

~ 32 ~

~ 33 ~

Letting go
gives others
the freedom
to be themselves.

~ 34 ~

~ 35 ~

Right before you open your eyes
that split second
before reality grips
hold of you
that is where peace reigns.

~ 36 ~

~ 37 ~

When a day's work is contained in a moment – time stands still

seconds, minutes and hours
lose their meaning

music, words and gestures blend onto
the horizon appeasing no one

day, dusk and dawn silently glide
along the horizon beckoning your awakening.

~ 38 ~

~ 39 ~

The stage turns dark
the light has gone on
to other pressing matters
leaving darkness
to fend for herself.

~ 40 ~

~ 41 ~

The wind tonight
peeps through
my window
watching me
thievishly
this opportunist
as l undress
my thoughts
lay them
naked beside
my drunken cup
spilled hopes and dreams
dripping from her rim.

~ 42 ~

~ 43 ~

Sweet as honey on a buttered bread
sour as a lemon drop melting away
the life we live in the here

calm as the sea, when the sun rises in the east
strong as a thunderstorm that catches you in the mist
the life we live in the here

quiet and peaceful as a stellar night
noisy and rough as a rush hour drive
the life we live in the here

the displays of these dominions are great,
but the oneness within is even greater.

~ 44 ~

~ 45 ~

Dust descending upon emptiness
dancing, embracing the void
creating by giving itself to
this vastness, a form still concealed
becoming the stone that will be sparked
by the light on its journey from long ago
creating life forces as of yet unknown,
new consciousness to explore
oh, creation of all that is
embrace me with your divine light
let my dust settle within this emptiness
on my way home.

~ 46 ~

~ 47 ~

How many mornings are there
within a day
how many moons can
sorrow hold in her embrace
how many sorrow filled breaths
does silence endure
then her lips break open
spilling all along the horizon.

~ 48 ~

~ 49 ~

Within the company of self
l find my heaven.

~ 50 ~

~ 51 ~

Letting go of someone
is not the same as losing them.

~ 52 ~

~ 53 ~

Who granted speech
the power to reach
immense heights while
within the same breath
devastating everything beneath?

~ 54 ~

~ 55 ~

What makes one person
hate so deeply and passionately
while another feels hatred's
sword carving away at the flesh.

~ 56 ~

~ 57 ~

On mornings when balance hangs
like an unaligned picture frame
in the room

l don't want to crawl out from
the comfort of my covers
these celestial walls beg me to stay

and let balance fend for herself.

~ 58 ~

~ 59 ~

On days when it is hard
getting out of one's own way
let everything come to you.

~ 60 ~

~ 61 ~

To struggle is a blessing
not yet unwrapped.

~ 62 ~

~ 63 ~

Between night and day
there is a fine line –
a change of perception
an open door
leading you on.

~ 64 ~

~ 65 ~

Mornings are like
unspoiled pages
and you are the
ink-dipped feather.

write something beautiful.

~ 66 ~

~ 67 ~

Life is like weaving a carpet
your creation of patterns
not visible
until your carpet is done.

~ 68 ~

~ 69 ~

Change when you've been asked to
so it won't come barreling down on you.

~ 70 ~

~ 71 ~

Heart beats
ring loudest
in solitary places.

~ 72 ~

~ 73 ~

Wherever you go
whatever you do
make sure you like
what is staring back at you.

~ 74 ~

~ 75 ~

At night
in bed
the day
revisits
hangs on
as if
not wanting
to exhale.

~ 76 ~

~ 77 ~

Where would l be
without the sweet
smell of morning.

~ 78 ~

~ 79 ~

Can you hear my whisper?
can you hear my calling?
I am everywhere...

l am in the falling rain
caressing your face
l am in the warmth
of the morning rays
l am in the cold
of a winter night
l am in your most
painful moments
l am in the sun
that warms your heart
I am in the soft touch
of your mate
l am in the tears that
roll down your cheek
l am in the smile
that you seek
l am that feeling
before thought

~ 80 ~

~ 81 ~

do you know who l am?

hold on to me
even if thought takes over
find me within you
and never let go
so that together
we can whisper to others
and show them the secrets
you just found.

~ 82 ~

~ 83 ~

Come sit with me
eat with me
drink with me
be with me
take me
but don't
break me.

~ 84 ~

~ 85 ~

We all have to find our way
some might get lost in the process
a bit more than others
but getting lost might be just what you needed.

~ 86 ~

~ 87 ~

Plan ahead
but be aware
that change might
interfere.

~ 88 ~

~ 89 ~

Be gently in all your encounters
even with the ones that bring rain.

~ 90 ~

~ 91 ~

Even in the poorest of places
you will find treasures enriching your life.

~ 92 ~

~ 93 ~

Sometimes l wait for morning
to come and fill my day.

~ 94 ~

~ 95 ~

Today l felt
light as a feather floating in the air

soon after

l crashed – hard like a falling rock
reality knew

just how to get a hold of me.

~ 96 ~

When I close my eyes
I can see
when I shut my ears
I can hear
when I surrender my thoughts
I can feel
when I stand still
I can journey
when I stop reaching
I am there
when I am silent
everything is speaking to me.

~ 98 ~

~ 99 ~

Spending time within the company of
self gives me the strength to be
within the company of others.

~ 100 ~

~ 101 ~

There is a place, far beyond these clouds
l visit in my dreams
just being their l want to stay
not having to return
the music there so full of us
comprised of many me's and you's
the absence of the spoken word
makes one complete.

~ 102 ~

~ 103 ~

I surrender to silent winged voices...
may l drink form your faith-giving goblet.

~ 104 ~

~ 105 ~

When rain pours down on you
dance in it.

~ 106 ~

~ 107 ~

We all cast shadows

~ 108 ~

~ 109 ~

Listen, come closer and listen
can you hear it?
relax and you will hear it
take a deep breath and...
hear it now... just faint... from far away
oh, what a sweet sound
let it fill your body and soul
that wonderful sweet sound of music
words... for your soul.

~ 110 ~

~ 111 ~

Be with me,
the tide says
l will teach you
the ancient ways
of time.

~ 112 ~

~ 113 ~

Invite morning to
be a guest
at your table.

~ 114 ~

~ 115 ~

I wanted to say
l am sorry for what I said...

   ...not for how l feel.

~ 116 ~

~ 117 ~

The world has fallen
silent between the both of us
but still, pain simmers on.

~ 118 ~

~ 119 ~

Your anger is looking
to crush my world,
so yours can remain standing.

~ 120 ~

~ 121 ~

The hardest thing
to let go of
are the closest ties
to your heart.

~ 122 ~

~ 123 ~

Be the buoy at sea
for all that look for safety.

~ 124 ~

~ 125 ~

Every new place I visit
is a wrapped present
begging me to look inside.

~ 126 ~

~ 127 ~

Winter – oh, strength within silence
Winter - oh, solitude of my soul
Winter - oh, stillness within my heart
Winter - oh, reflection of peace
Winter - oh, rejuvenation of spirit
Winter - oh, restored balance upon me

Strengthen me - so l can abide spring.

~ 128 ~

~ 129 ~

We pray – before we lay our head to rest
We pray – to the sun rising in the east
We pray – in churches small
We pray – in big cathedrals
We pray – within the city
We pray – alone
We pray – in groups
We pray – in sorrow
We pray – for thanks
But who does hear you... when you pray?

YOU DO!

~ 130 ~

~ 131 ~

Tick tock, tick tock, this constant pulse
we wake to it, we sleep to it
this rhythm never stops

we live by it, we die by it
we love to it, we hate to it
this rhythm of the clock

in tiny segments we devour hour after hour
tick tock, tick tock, a never-ending hourglass
sand running through my fist

this constant tick, followed by tock
they reign in unison
the waters rising to its clock

tick tock tick tock, this rhythm never slows
its beat is constant, never yields
this rhythm of the clock

but then one day it stops
tick tock tick tock, the hourglass of mine - ran out of time.

~ 132 ~

~ 133 ~

Day and night
darkness and brightness
good and bad
love and hate
big and small
happy and sad
sun and rain
empty and full
peace and war
you and me

all aspects of two things and yet
    contained within one.

~ 134 ~

~ 135 ~

A soft gentle touch
a kiss on the cheek

out of the east

then he glides on
past the dunes

leaving me smiling in the mist.

~ 136 ~

~ 137 ~

Daybreaks
brief visits

unable to cross
the threshold

introverts with
immense auras

giving us
a brief look

into their world.

~ 138 ~

~ 139 ~

Dreams of my solitary nights within
the renderings of illusions brought to light

vividly within the imagination of my mind
so that the moment that I wake

my hands can form and render what my
mind created in the solitude of my being.

~ 140 ~

~ 141 ~

When one door closes another stands ajar
unsure of what lies beyond its sill

forward motion propels on to step across
you may swim – you may drown

faith is beckoning

        are you listening?

~ 142 ~

~ 143 ~

Darkness only remains in the
absence of light

light emits truth, reveals shadows,
in her absence not even shadows remain

shadows are the remnants of darkness

dim light creates large shadows
but when the light burns bright and strong

no shadows will remain.

~ 144 ~

~ 145 ~

The view is clearest
after rain.

~ 146 ~

~ 147 ~

We all need mornings to
gently kiss us on our cheeks.

~ 148 ~

~ 149 ~

Love is the tears
in your eyes
when saying goodbye.

~ 150 ~

~ 151 ~

Your love showed me
that there is such a thing
which makes me quiver and tremble
when you open my door.

~ 152 ~

~ 153 ~

Love everything
and
everything will
love you
back.

~ 154 ~

~ 155 ~

There is no you or us or them
in these far-off places

the need for individuality nonexistent

there is no I or you in LOVE.

~ 156 ~

~ 157 ~

Love is the ointment
mending the heart.

~ 158 ~

~ 159 ~

Love is
but for
the sake
of love
not hatred
or denial
can render
her speechless
love is
by definition
the breath
we draw.

~ 160 ~

~ 161 ~

The thing that made
you fall in love with me
is the same thing
that made you fall
out of love with me.

~ 162 ~

~ 163 ~

My love
unanswered

my words
unheard

my deeds
unacknowledged

empty are
the spaces between

a cup without bottom
can hold nothing in

but still l keep giving
hoping a drop will stick to its rim.

~ 164 ~

~ 165 ~

My love encumbers everything

you and me and the whole spectrum

that is filled within me of all that

l am and ever will be.

~ 166 ~

~ 167 ~

The painter's brush touched by the deep silence of reality, brings
forth onto the barren, naked canvas, illuminations past
the reach of language

the poet's feather sparked by far off places
the essence of totality brings into being from the oceans
of emptiness, the illumination within

the musician, moved within the silence of his soul
can reach up high above the clouds on the horizon
and into spaces deep within the listener's fortified heart

the lovers' benevolent embrace that reaches deep within to blend
two souls as one, can make the heavens fuse and render
igniting the stars to burst into new light

the gift of silence to humanity
awakening of the heavens within to rejoice
with the heavens above.

~ 168 ~

~ 169 ~

Everything that is

is not

everything that is not

in essence is.

~ 170 ~

~ 171 ~

Home...

no address reveals its existence
no space that defines this place

home...

no walls that cherish possessions
no windows that hamper your sight

home...

no roof that keeps you from seeing the stars
no basement filled with relics

home...

the feeling within, your burning flame
close your eyes and you are home.

~ 172 ~

~ 173 ~

The curtain is no longer drawn
light enters – revealing
what lies within

for all to see

ghost-like shadows
held so tight – remnants
of past expressions

cast from the podium

to reign the forest
of another world – not
yet revealed.

~ 174 ~

~ 175 ~

Subtle and humble morning came
shy to introduce herself
the bride of mornings delight
the way she it up the room

made me complete.

~ 176 ~

Yesterday, today and tomorrow
are but one
contained within the now

yesterday a dream
today an illusion
tomorrow never comes.

~ 178 ~

~ 179 ~

Events
Give way to faded memories

leaves
turn colors, fall away

both
like glue- bound pages

whitter
in the garden

of my thoughts.

~ 180 ~

~ 181 ~

Unity
invited me
to see
that even
within chaos
perfection reigns.

~ 182 ~

~ 183 ~

Care for all that is entrusted to you
care for what is deep inside of you
care for what is given to you

and the world will care for you.

~ 184 ~

~ 185 ~

The greatest gift
to soul is silence
so her faint calling
can travel to your ear.

~ 186 ~

~ 187 ~

The tide rolls in so softly
and l become her ripples rolling in.

~ 188 ~

~ 189 ~

Voices within the depth of one's own
igniting the vastness of creation

sparked by the soul to carry the flame
that transforms the world into being

this gift from the past for the here and now
which is given to what is yet to come

oh depthless within, fill me to the rim
so l can drown in the vastness of my being.

$\sim$ 190 $\sim$

~ 191 ~

My first love
was a puddle
my second love
was a lake
my third love
was the sea
my fourth love
was a storm
my fifth love
was the love for self
drowning all others.

~ 192 ~

~ 193 ~

I am the sum of all my experiences
which made me who l am today
and even within my darkest of places
there shines a faint light.

~ 194 ~

~ 195 ~

Happiness
is a one way street.

~ 196 ~

~ 197 ~

Sorrow creeps up slowly
sneaking in through the back door

making a home for herself
shadows appear where there once was

light, oozing smells of death drips from
her veins coating my hopes and dreams.

~ 198 ~

~ 199 ~

When you find a place
undisturbed by man
time loses its meaning

when you sit in silence
among nature
all becomes one

and when you find the
butterfly garden within
you are home.

~ 200 ~

~ 201 ~

Why does the spoken word
reign sovereign
baring sentiments
to inhabit the twilight.

~ 202 ~

~ 203 ~

Solitary mornings come
and they do go.

~ 204 ~

~ 205 ~

Full moon
tide changing
sleep interrupted

full moon – awakens my heart.

~ 206 ~

~ 207 ~

The day returns to me
what the night has stolen.

~ 208 ~

~ 209 ~

I wish l could
heal your wounds
so you don't have
to feel pain.

~ 210 ~

~ 211 ~

Love deeply
love silently
love everything
so love can endure.

www.ingramcontent.com/pod-product-compliance
Lightning Source LLC
Chambersburg PA
CBHW060915120626
46553CB00001B/338